Revised Edition

Jeff Gordon

By Jeff Savage

Lerner Publications Company/Minneapolis

Copyright © 2007 by Jeff Savage

All rights reserved. International copyright secured. No part of this book may be reproduced, stored in a retrieval system, or transmitted in any form or by any means—electronic, mechanical, photocopying, recording, or otherwise—without the prior written permission of Lerner Publishing Group, Inc., except for the inclusion of brief quotations in an acknowledged review.

Lerner Publications Company
A division of Lerner Publishing Group, Inc.
241 First Avenue North
Minneapolis, MN 55401 U.S.A.

Website address: www.lernerbooks.com

Library of Congress Cataloging-in-Publication Data

Savage, Jeff, 1961—
Jeff Gordon / by Jeff Savage. — Rev. ed.
p. cm. — (Amazing athletes)
Includes bibliographical references and index.
ISBN-13: 978-0-8225-6802-5 (lib. bdg. : alk. paper)
ISBN-10: 0-8225-6802-0 (lib. bdg. : alk. paper)
1. Gordon, Jeff, 1971—Juvenile literature. 2. Automobile racing drivers—United States—Biography—Juvenile literature. I. Title. II. Series.
GV1032.G67 S275 2007
796.72092—dc21 2006013846

Manufactured in the United States of America
3 4 5 6 7 8 – BP – 13 12 11 10 09 08

Table of Contents

A Fast Ride 4

Built for Speed 8

Sprinting to the Lead 11

Into the Big Time 15

Winning the Race 22

Selected Career Highlights 29

Glossary 30

Further Reading & Websites 31

Index 32

Jeff Gordon's well-known Chevy race car carries the number 24. It also has stickers on it from a lot of different companies.

A Fast Ride

Jeff Gordon's number 24 car zipped down the track. At speeds close to 100 miles per hour, the colorful machine was just a blur. Jeff and 42 other drivers were battling for the **checkered flag** at the 2006 Dodge/Save Mart 350. The contest was at Infineon Raceway in Sonoma,

California. Jeff was born less than 20 miles from the track. He had already won four races at Infineon.

This race was also special to Jeff for another reason. He had just told friends and family about his engagement. He was going to be married to girlfriend Ingrid Vandebosch.

Jeff had been behind other drivers for most of the race. But he stayed close to the leaders. By **lap** 70 of the 110-lap race,

Uniform on, Jeff is almost ready to race!

After a slow start, Jeff takes the lead at the 2006 Dodge/Save Mart 350.

Jeff was only 12 seconds behind the leader, Terry Labonte. Labonte was running low on gas and had to slow his speed.

This was the chance that Jeff had been waiting for. He squeezed the steering wheel tightly and focused on the car in front of him. By lap 88, Jeff was ready to make his move. On a sharp turn of the track, he moved his car to the inside and zoomed past Labonte. Jeff took the lead and never looked back. "I'm speechless," said Jeff after the race. "What an amazing moment this is, a very special weekend for me and this race team to get back to victory lane."

The victory was just another highlight in an amazing career. Jeff Gordon, one of the best race car drivers in the world, had done it again.

Jeff celebrates another victory at Infineon. The 2006 Dodge/Save Mart 350 was Jeff's fifth victory at the track.

Jeff got his first taste of racing at a young age. His stepfather brought home a quarter midget car like this one.

Built for Speed

Jeff has been racing vehicles ever since he can remember. He was born in 1971 in Vallejo, California. Jeff's father left home when Jeff was just three months old. Jeff's sister, Kim, was three years old at the time. Jeff was four in 1975, when his mother, Carol, remarried.

Jeff's new stepfather's name was John Bickford. Jeff called him Dad.

That same year, Jeff learned to ride a BMX bike. He practiced tricks on a track at the end of the street. Jeff's mother didn't think this type of biking was safe.

When Jeff's father bought him a race car, Jeff forgot all about his BMX bike. At first, Jeff's mom was shocked. Then she figured out that racing cars was actually safer then biking—even though the driver was only four years old!

Jeff's race car was a **quarter midget**. It was about six feet long and painted black. The fastest it could go was twenty miles per hour.

Jeff and his father cleared the weeds from a nearby field. Jeff practiced driving nearly every day.

By the age of five, Jeff was racing his quarter midget against older children at local California tracks. A year later, he began competing in **go-karts** that went twice as fast. At seven, he started playing video games, which helped him develop quick **reflexes**.

Jeff's quarter midget had his nickname "Gordy" painted on the hood.

Dark-haired and soft-spoken, Jeff was small for his age. By third grade, kids began teasing him. Jeff feared the bullies, but he never let them know it. A few times, he even defended himself in fights. Before long, the bullying stopped.

SECTION JG

SATURDAY
SPORTS REVIEW

June 9, 1979

J

Speedy youngster becomes Quarter Midget Champion!

Jeff won his first quarter midget national championship in 1979.

Sprinting to the Lead

Jeff listened to his teachers and earned good grades in school. His reward was more racing. He and his father traveled to racetracks all over California.

In 1979, when Jeff was eight, he became the quarter midget national champion for the first time. He was competing against drivers who were twice his age. By 1981, Jeff was entering local races against teenagers. He won every race.

Sprint cars were Jeff's next challenge. He began racing them in 1983.

By the age of twelve, Jeff began practicing in a half-ton **sprint car** with a powerful 600-**horsepower** engine. But drivers had to be at least fourteen years old to compete in sprint races. Jeff tried to sneak into races by making himself look older. He drew a phony mustache on his face with an eyebrow pencil. Sometimes the trick worked, and Jeff got to race. Other times, the race officials sent him home.

Sprint racing was harder for Jeff. The other drivers were very skilled. One time, Jeff and his father traveled to Florida for a big race. Jeff's car broke down on the very first lap. Jeff cried and wished he could quit racing. But his father wouldn't let him give up.

Jeff and his father grew tired of trying to sneak into races. They learned that many racetracks in the central United States had no age limits. So in 1984, when Jeff was thirteen, his family moved to Pittsboro, Indiana. There he could compete in any race he wanted.

Outside Pittsboro is a sign that reads: "Pittsboro Welcomes you, The Hometown of Jeff Gordon, NASCAR Driver."

Within a year, Jeff won his first sprint car race. It was at K-C Raceway in Chillcothe, Ohio. When Jeff crossed the finish line, he cried tears of joy. His father ran down the hill to the center of the track. He hugged Jeff and lifted him high in the air.

In May 1990, Jeff's car edged past the car of Rich Vogler. Rich was one of Jeff's earliest rivals.

Jeff's dad *(far right)* helped Jeff celebrate winning both the sprint and midget championships in 1990.

Into the Big Time

Jeff's favorite subject in high school was science, because he learned more about how an engine works. Jeff raced most weekends and sometimes used Fridays to travel. This meant he missed school, but he always made up the work. For fun with his friends, he shot pool, skateboarded, and played video games.

Jeff poses for his graduation picture. He was about to graduate from Tri-West High School in Lizton, Indiana.

Jeff stayed in shape by running on the cross-country team of Tri-West High School. But racing was easily his favorite sport. He even competed in a race on the night of his graduation

Jeff's racing helped make him popular in high school. The other students voted him prom king during his senior year.

from Tri-West in 1989. He began competing in stock car racing soon after, when he joined the Busch Grand National circuit. He teamed with **pit crew** chief Ray Evernham.

On the Busch Grand National circuit, Jeff drove a white Ford. It carried the logo of Baby Ruth candy bars.

The Busch circuit is part of **NASCAR**, which stands for National Association for Stock Car Auto Racing. Stock cars are like regular cars that people drive on roads, except they have bigger engines. NASCAR holds races each year at tracks across the United States. Drivers collect points based on how well they race. At the end of the season, the driver with the most points wins the **points title** and the NASCAR championship.

At Hendrick Motorsports, Jeff's car had its own shop and fifteen mechanics. They wore very colorful overalls. The clothes earned them the nickname, the "Rainbow Warriors."

Jeff burst onto the NASCAR scene as a daredevil racer. In 1992, he won a record eleven **pole positions** and three victories.

A **sponsor** named Rick Hendrick was so impressed that he offered to help pay some of Jeff's expenses. In exchange, Hendrick Motorsports would get some of the **prize money**. Hendrick's company was based in Charlotte, North Carolina. Jeff and his parents moved there later in 1992.

Rick Hendrick *(left)* and Jeff have enjoyed a solid relationship since 1992.

The next step up from the Busch circuit was the Winston Cup circuit. Jeff became the Winston Cup Rookie of the Year in 1993.

In 1993, Jeff became a rookie on the Winston Cup circuit—the top level of NASCAR. The day before the Daytona 500 in Florida, Jeff competed in the 125-mile **qualifying race** against the best stock car racers in the world. Jeff shocked everyone by winning the race. Afterward, he met Miss Winston, Brooke Sealey. Jeff and Brooke soon began dating. A year later, they were married.

Brooke Sealey was a student at the University of North Carolina when she met Jeff in 1993.

Throughout the 1990s, Jeff raced against NASCAR's best drivers. These included Dale Earnhardt, who drove his famous number 3 Chevy.

Winning the Race

Jeff won his first points race in the middle of the 1994 NASCAR season at the Coca-Cola 600 in Charlotte. Afterward, Jeff told reporters: "This is the greatest moment of my life, a feeling I will never forget." Six weeks later, Jeff won his second race. The next day, he read in the newspaper that he'd been given a nickname, "The Kid."

Jeff holds up a trophy for winning his first Brickyard 400 in 1994.

Jeff signs autographs for a few of his millions of fans.

Jeff roared out front in 1995 and never looked back. He cruised to his first Winston Cup points title to become the youngest champion of the modern era. Jeff was a famous celebrity. Companies created Jeff Gordon souvenir T-shirts, caps, sunglasses, key chains, coffee mugs, and yo-yos.

Jeff enjoyed his popularity, but he ignored all the fuss and concentrated on winning. He won ten races in 1996 to earn $3.5 million in prize money. Then he won ten more races in 1997 and claimed his second points title. Jeff was determined to become even better. But how could he possibly top two ten-win seasons in a row? By winning thirteen times!

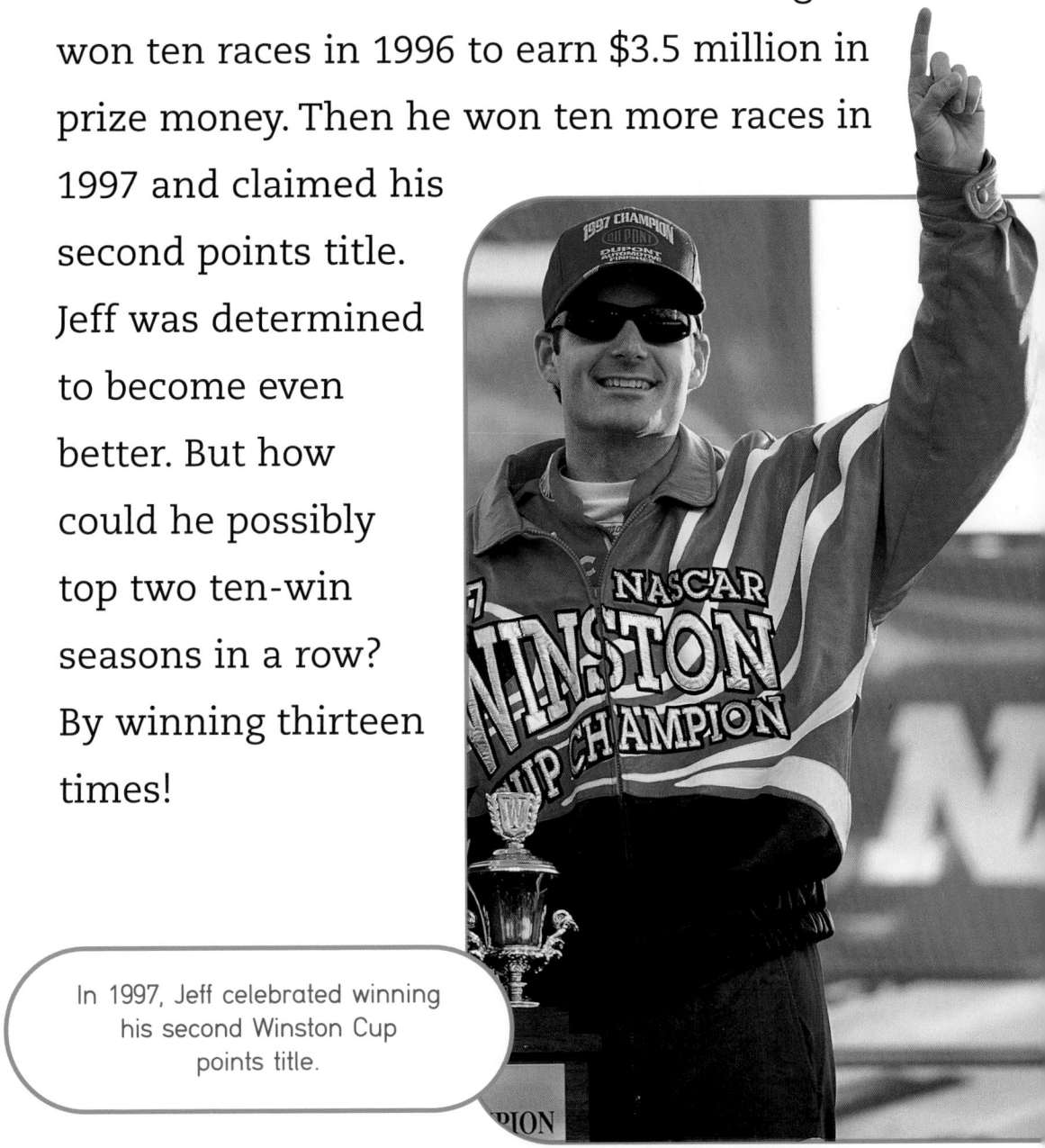

In 1997, Jeff celebrated winning his second Winston Cup points title.

Jeff tied the modern record in 1998 for most wins in a season. "I have to admit," Jeff said, "that at my age, you're not expected to do all this. It's amazing to me I've gotten this far."

In the early 2000s, Jeff faced some challenges. He and pit crew chief Ray Evernham parted ways. Throughout the 2000 racing season, Jeff struggled without Ray. He won three times and placed ninth in the points standings. Jeff and his new pit crew chief, Robbie Loomis, worked hard to improve Jeff's car.

Jeff has come to rely on the skills of his pit crew chief, Robbie Loomis.

The speed of the Rainbow Warriors in the pit helped Jeff capture his third Brickyard 400 victory in 2001.

The hard work paid off in 2001, when Jeff roared to his fourth Winston Cup points title. His favorite victory was his third win at the Brickyard 400, the day after his thirtieth birthday. The next year, though, Brooke and Jeff separated, and Brooke filed for divorce.

A young fan asks Jeff a question at a Kids and the Hood event.

In 2002, Jeff was the youngest driver to win sixty races. He followed up that honor by earning the Nextel Cup points title for the fifth time in 2004. His wins since then have made him motorsports' all-time money winner. But Jeff gives back too. He created an organization called Kids and the Hood that helps children.

Jeff's message to kids is simple: "Don't Ever Quit." When it comes to racing, fans know that Jeff Gordon won't ever quit.

Selected Career Highlights

2007 Finished second in Sprint Cup Series points

2006 Won fifth race at Infineon Raceway

2005 Finished 11th in Nextel Cup points

2004 Won Nextel Cup points title

2003 Finished fourth in Winston Cup points

2002 Won his sixtieth race, youngest driver ever to do so

2001 Won fourth Winston Cup points title, only third driver to do so
Became first NASCAR driver to win more than $10 million in one year

2000 Became the youngest Winston Cup driver in history to win fifty races
Set record with six straight road course wins

1999 Won seven Winston Cup races
Was first-ever driver to win the most races five years in a row

1998 Won Winston Cup points title

1997 Won Winston Cup points title
Became the youngest driver ever to win the Daytona 500

1996 Finished second overall in Winston Cup points

1995 Won his first Winston Cup points title, youngest driver to do so

1994 Won his first Brickyard 400 race at Indianapolis Motor Speedway

1993 Named Winston Cup Rookie of the Year

1992 Moved up from Busch Grand National to Winston Cup circuit

1991 Won National Dirt Track Championship

1990 Won USAC Midget Championship

GLOSSARY

checkered flag: the black-and-white flag that is waved at the end of a race

go-kart: a small, flat, one-person vehicle with a motor that is used for racing (called karting)

horsepower: a measure of an engine's power; the greater the horsepower, the faster the car

lap: one complete go-around on a racetrack. A NASCAR race typically is made up of hundreds of laps.

NASCAR: the National Association for Stock Car Auto Racing. Founded in 1947, NASCAR is the governing group of stock-car racing. It says which changes to a car's engine and body allow it to keep its "stock car" status.

pit crew: a team of mechanics that works on a car during a pit stop. A pit stop happens when the driver pulls off the racetrack and his or her car is adjusted and refueled.

points title: an award given each year to the NASCAR driver who has earned the most points throughout the racing season

pole position: the inside front row—the best position—at the start of a race. The driver who gets this position was the fastest in the qualifying race held before the real race.

prize money: the money awarded to each driver based on the driver's finish in a race

qualifying race: a race that takes place before the real race to determine the starting order of all the cars. The fastest car in the qualifying race wins the pole position for the real race.

quarter midget: a race car that is larger than a go-kart but smaller than a sprint car

reflexes: automatic responses, done without thinking

sponsor: someone who pays for a driver's car, pit crew, travel, and other expenses in return for a share of the driver's prize winnings. The driver also pastes the sponsor's logo all over the race car as a form of advertising.

sprint car: a race car that is larger than a quarter midget but smaller than a stock car. It has a powerful engine.

FURTHER READING & WEBSITES

Bradley, Michael. *Jeff Gordon.* New York: Benchmark, 2003.

Christopher, Matt. *On the Track with Jeff Gordon.* New York: Little Brown & Company, 2001.

Gigliotti, Jim. *Jeff Gordon: Simply the Best.* Chanhassen, MN: Child's World, 2002.

Johnstone, Mike. *NASCAR.* Minneapolis, MN: Lerner Publications Company, 2002.

Kirkpatrick, Rob. *Jeff Gordon: Nascar Champion.* New York: Powerkids Press, 2000.

MacNow, Glen. *Jeff Gordon.* Berkeley Heights, NJ: Enslow Publishers, 2001.

Sherman, Josepha. *Jeff Gordon.* Crystal Lake, IL: Heinemann Library, 2001.

Jeff Gordon Online
http://www.gordonline.com
A fan website that gives loads of information not only about Jeff but also about the Hendrick Motorsports team and general NASCAR information and links.

NASCAR Website
http://www.nascar.com
A website developed by NASCAR that provides fans with recent news stories, biographies of drivers, and information about racing teams and race cars.

The Official Website
http://www.jeffgordon.com
Jeff's official website, featuring games, trivia, photos, and information about auto racing.

Sports Illustrated for Kids
http://www.sikids.com
The *Sports Illustrated for Kids* website that covers all sports, including auto racing.

INDEX

Bickford, Carol (mother), 8, 9, 19
Bickford, John, (stepfather), 8, 9, 10, 11, 13, 14, 15, 19
Brickyard 400, 4, 5, 6, 23, 27
Busch Grand National circuit, 17, 18

Daytona 500, 20

Evernham, Ray, 17, 26

go-karts, 10
Gordon, Jeff: achievements of, 5, 7, 11, 14, 18, 21, 22, 23, 24, 25, 26, 28, 29; early life of, 8–14; earnings of, 25, 28; personal life of, 10, 15, 16, 21, 22, 28; and school, 11, 15, 16
Gordon, Kim (sister), 8

Hendrick Motorsports, 18, 19
Hendrick, Rick, 19

Infineon Raceway, 4–7

Loomis, Robbie, 26

NASCAR, 18, 20, 22
Nextel Cup, 28

quarter midgets, 8, 9, 10, 11

Rainbow Warriors, 18, 27

Sealey, Brooke, 21, 27
sprint cars, 12–14

Winston Cup championships, 24, 25, 27
Winston Cup circuit, 20

PHOTO ACKNOWLEDGMENTS

Photos reproduced with the permission of: © Craig Jones/Allsport/Getty Images, pp. 4, 29; © Streeter Lecka/Getty Images, p. 5; © Chris Stanford/Getty Images, pp. 6, 7; © Stephanie Maze/CORBIS, p. 8; © Bill Hauser/Independent Picture Service, p. 11; © John Mahoney, pp. 12, 14, 15; © Classmates.com Yearbook Archives, p. 16; © SportsChrome East/West/Greg Crisp, pp. 17, 20, 21, 24; © Scott McNair, M.D., pp. 19, 26, 27; © Robert LaBerge/Allsport/Getty Images, p. 22; © James Cutler, p. 23; © SportsChrome East/West, p. 25; © Tom Raymond, courtesy DuPont Company, p. 28.

Cover: © David Taylor/Allsport/Getty Images (top); © Scott McNair, M.D. (bottom).